For all your broken pieces. A reminder of the extraordinary beauty within your bruised soul.

At Dawn

She will emblazon your soul with embers of a
wandering wildfire.

Igniting every sense, encouraging you with gentle
laughter to dance within her flames.

In a brilliant flash all you will be left with is the aroma
of black smoke and suffocating ashes.

Your only reminder she was ever there. Don't be fooled
by the dawn, every sun must set into the eve.

Summer

Vibrant.

Bold.

Soft.

Rich.

The morning skies alight with a rusted orange glow.

The afternoons a silent blistering blue.

The evening's water colored with periwinkle, lavender and rose.

People floating under the stars. People filled with ever changing pallets.

Desire. Anger. Frustration. Joy. Curiosity.
All omitting waves of pulsating color.

The warmth of dew drops settling on the skin. The simple painting of a Summer Dawn.

A Time Before

I remember the time before my wounds.

Alabaster skin untouched.

Unloved.

Perfection without a heartbeat.

I remember my body before pain.

Vaguely.

A searing immortality pulsing through fragile veins.

Melodies of a time before I came alive. Calm waters before the
storm that shaped me.

I remember a time before my wounds.

A memory nothing more.

In His Eyes

Amber, green, an ocean of blue, black as the starless sky.

Peering into eyes is to travel through the universe
discovering every star.

You reminded me that all we are is dust.

Ordinary and extraordinary all at once.

Stillness

Flaxen fields unmoving in the heavy humidity of dusk.

The only sounds are the whimpers of coyotes, the sigh of the trees, the chattering of owls.

My skin feels less my own.

More of the stars.

Kissed by citrus pollen.

There is a rhythm in stillness.

A steady beating of drums.

A reminder of our impermanence, a testament to how we belong to nature above all else.

Our toes should be buried in the Earth, our hair windblown with petals laced into every strand.

Our lips as sweet as honeysuckle.

Our fingertips smelling of wild jasmine.

Our eyes beaming with the light of the moon.

There is nothing more than this right here. This is enough. This is everything.

Be still.

Golden Light

Love has a way of wilting or blooming,

When your eyes begin to flutter.

The nature of loving,

Is freedom.

It's defiance that is as strong as it is delicate.

It does not rest in the light or dark.

It makes a home somewhere in between.

Love, smells of lemongrass after a tropical rain.

Intoxicating. Seductive. Yet Familiar.

Love will always bring pain.

You will have wounds deeper than the black holes

Lurking in the depth of the seas we have yet to explore.

But they will make you glow with life in remembrance of how they came to be.

You will love many hearts.

You will become woven into countless souls.

Let it all in.

Take the wounds.

Nourish them with your tears.

Become love.

A radiant beam of perplexing light that never ceases to shine.

Even when the darkness falls.

You are the golden beam of sunset.

The sleeping dandelion.

The kiss of lightning during a thunderstorm.

You are love.

Remain

Follow the clouds.

Leap from one to the next.

Delicate. Soft. Steady.

Ignore the ticking of the clocks surrounding you.

It is a fantasy. Nothing more.

Time is fluid. Muted. Ever changing.

Faster. Slower. Stopping and starting.

Savor the sticky sweetness of a summer ripened fig.

Let the harvest of tomatoes from your vines sit in your hands.

Lean down and breathe in the intoxicating aroma.

You can run as fast as sound and you still won't be able to
change the outcome of your life.

You will get there.

Each step leading you to the place you were always meant to be.

Each illness, every heartbreak, every career that didn't fit...

It is molding you. Readying you for all that is yet to come.

Remain here.

In the present.

Be with the clouds, not the clocks.

Dandelion Greens

Bitterness.

A tingling on the tongue. A pursing of the lips.

Not all of life could possibly be sweet.

We crave a balanced palate.

Bloom

Kaleidoscope of radiant color.

She is the reflection of light, the flash at the edge of the horizon.

The way she rises at the dawn makes even the sun envious of her warmth.

Happiness blooms within as you fall even deeper in love with her enigmatic, fractured soul.

More Then Flesh

The shedding of skin happens in the depth of shadow.

Leaving remnants of flesh behind.

The caverns of pain are endless. The gaping wounds a reminder
of our fragile mortality.

We are more than flesh and bone. More than our physical pain.
More than our shattering of pieces.

Even the gravest cut will heal.

So will you my love.

So will you.

Flame

Burning like a wildfire was all I knew how to do.

Passion.

Movement.

Bursting from the seams of my soul.

Time moved on, the fire

Burned,

Burned,

Burned, away.

Midnight stars ablaze. Flames cooling softly, slowly.

Everyday a desire for embers.

Teardrops from the sky.

A knowing that my fervor for life could exist with more profound strength if I learned to simmer the flames within.

A glowing splinter smoldering in the ashes. Flickers of golden light.

The power of flames, contained, nurtured, reserved for a time and place they are deeply needed.

Instead of the raging red of fire become…

The soft yellow of a dandelion.

The color of life rather than devastation.

Become…

A promise of the continuation of living despite the imminent coming of grief and heartache.

Burn my darling.

For a lover.

For a dream.

Light flames of inspiration.

You are forever an ember, a raindrop, a blooming flower in spring, the dust of the cosmos.

You embody it all.

Awaken.

Succumb.

Learn.

Transform.

Near Light

There is no other way to describe the warmth of your body
pressed against mine.

Being near you is being near light.

The Sway of a Woman

The sheer strength of a woman can be found in her enduring heart, her undeniable fortitude, the quiet knowing of her mind, the fervent curiosity, effortless sensuality and her uncanny ability to

Rise

From

The

Ashes.

Painting

She was created to be painted. Every curve and edge to be explored.

Calendula laced, sun kissed skin. Lashes touched with dandelion blossoms.

Scars that become kisses strewn across a blank canvas.

Her soul only half complete.

Begging for color, burning covet for touch.

Broken and whole.

Broken and whole.

A painting yet to be imagined.

Juniper

Sweeter than honey. Juniper smoke is captivating. The aroma delicious, enticing, seductive in its pure beauty.

Inhale.

The sweet perfume of wild sage after a long awaited rain.

Strange and familiar.

The nights I could not sleep. Steeped in aches and fear of not waking to the sunrise.

I sat outside under a blanket of stars. Juniper ripe on the breeze.

A scent of home. A tale of tomorrow. A catalyst to live for today.

A miracle only nature can provide.

A smell that breathes life.

At Dusk

Laughter.

Calm and sweet.

A plum. Purple, sticky with pliable flesh that ripens
with the gentlest touch.

My soul was awakened by the sound of your
melodious voice. Dancing on the cotton candy sky
of your dreams.

Eyes. The color of earth and wind combined. Eyes I
instantly knew. Eyes I couldn't tear myself away
from. Sound faded.

We fell together. Puzzle pieces that had longed to be
woven.

Our love, like dusk was not meant to last forever.

Not in this life.

In another time, another world our souls danced as
the sun set beneath the ocean.

And after that last kiss and the taste of plum...

We left our love at twilight.

Grow

The crisp winds of winter fall into the pulsating growth of spring.

Summer comes with the piercing heat. Heat that suffocates and inspires nostalgia for youth and long forgotten love.

Autumn. Sweet autumn. A time often seen as the beginning of death. And yet look at the abundance of colors, the rosiness of women's cheeks, the romance of cinnamon and nutmeg sprinkled on the breeze.

The seasons remind us that our live is constantly in transition. Moving. Ebbing. Flowing.

The desire to stay still. To stand in a moment and relive a smile, a feeling, a gentle touch. It calls us deeply. Stay. Stay here and do not let time consume you.

But we cannot stay. Even when we want to. Even when it means letting go of people and places we love so dearly.

We must allow our roots to become unhinged. The wind to carry us. The caressing of new earth, the hands of new love, the sound of new voices.

We are capable of so much more than we will ever know. Capable of greatness within adversity. Capable of enduring the gravest pain.

When you forget your own ability to move forward. Look to the seasons. The way they come and go. Seamlessly allowing themselves to change. Year after year. Day after day.

Falling in love with the transition.

The Silence

Words often mean nothing.

The less we say the more we come to know.

It is in the subtle movement of a hand.

The flutter of eyelashes.

The sweetness of a smile.

It is in the prickles on the skin, the way a body leans into or
away from another.

Some things require no words.

Most moments require listening not just with our ears but our
souls.

In the moments of silence we can discover hidden treasure.

The gift of another, in all our tarnished glory.

Raw

I want to see you broken.

A million pieces cascading on the breeze.

I want to see your fragments, your scars, your blemishes, tears and unadulterated joy.

I want your hair wild and untamed.

Your skin alive from the chill in the air. Your eyes lit from the life pulsating within.

Give me the sinners.

Give me the people that don't give to get a better world but out of the knowledge that this life right now is all we have.

Give me the people who wear scars as bright as the stars in the blackened sky.

Darling, give me you.

Raw and unaltered.

Let me love all of your broken dreams, the trauma of illness, the agony of grief.

Let me remind you that your magnificence comes from the brilliance of your mind, the sway of your hips, the melody of your laughter.

It comes from the way your touch heals the ones you love. Strip yourself bare. What's left?

Raw.

Earth

I lie on the cold, wet earth.

Staring upward.

Watching the evening sky fade into the orange blossom of sunrise.

I tell myself all is well.

Inhale. Exhale.

I am still here.

I can still love.

I can still feel the blood coursing through my body.

I am somebody's harvest and they are mine.

This is enough to hold me across the cosmos.

It's Okay

All that we can do

Breathe.

Love.

Give.

Learn.

Grow.

Until we are called to the next life.

It's okay to sit in the dark.

It's okay to cry.

It's okay to be utterly angry at the delicacy of your human form…

It's okay dear heart.

Lilacs

In between the rhythmic beats your sweetness lingered.

Your voice became a home.

It sounded like the purple sky.

Scattered with illuminating light.

There was no way to put into words the way my soul fell into yours.

Dew drops on springs first lilacs.

That is how I loved you.

Crave

When a body fails it becomes primal with desire.

Cravings for human flesh, the sweetness of cherry stained lips.

Following the freckles on cheeks until night falls.

Then in the depth of darkness remembering every curve of a body, every dimple... the sound of a smile echoes.

These pleasures so often forgotten to those who forget we are on borrowed time.

Holding springs flowers becomes a celebration. An ode to life in all its splendor.

Holding you... Every craving of this frail human body fulfilled.

Fragments

Bruised veins giving the sweet metallic nectar of life.

Pain teaches you that every heartbeat is a mystery.

It is not yours alone.

It is a teacher.

A murderer.

A friend.

A foe.

Autumn

Your breathing is gentle now.

I read to you. I read about the falling leaves of autumn. The crispness of the bitter wind. Rose colored cheeks and echoes of laughter.

The first bite of a tart apple. Carvings of Pumpkins and the feeling of wool jumpers on bare skin.

I look up between words. Every piece of you different yet the same.

Memorizing your eyelashes…and then as my lips speak of fireworks at dusk, you smile.

It is like being hit by one million stars. To see you smile. To see you remember if even for a moment the life before this chapter.

I know you will have fireworks as you write your next story. As your body leaves this world, you will become the beam of light you have always been. The bitter chill we lived for. The soft woolen jumper. The snowflakes on eyelashes.

This is only the beginning of the greatest adventure we will know my love. Go softly. Be well. See you soon.

Whispers

Poignant words need not be spoken loud.

Love not proclaimed with fire and zest.

Grief not in fits of tears and screams of agony.

Sometimes all that is needed is whispers.

Roots

She was made of wild things.

Hair that never settled, flying upward with the slightest breeze.

Eyes that darted here and there, never settling on one focal point.

She was a rider of the wind, sailor of the seas. Roots were a foreign thought.

An elusive concept placing oneself in the ground, the commitment of staying in one place to grow.

Terrifying and yet oddly desired.

Balance.

Find a way to ride the wind and bury oneself all at once.

Earth and air intertwined into a world of luster.

Flower of the Field

When my life became moments of darkness I did not recognize. When I found solace in another's arms just to escape the reality of my every day.

My life sworn into black and white. The deepest depths of an endless ocean. The numbness of loss. A cavern black as night. I am drowning. Shallow edges deceive me. I feel your movements inside of me. I feel your heartbeat. Then in the blink of my tired eyes you are gone again.

From your once fluttering heartbeat I lost track of my own. A million facets of me floating into beams of light. Looking down upon my own devastated body.

Fetal position on a cold, damp floor. Covered in the saltiness of my own tears.

There is life yet, in this body and in this soul. Life to be created. Love to be given. And you, my flower of the field.

You broke me as much as you built me. And yet you were created in a time where my body had only known emptiness. The shattering of my being was a reminder that I was alive. That I could, despite all the loss create LIFE. That in despair, I could endure. You my darling child are the greatest teacher. The most beautiful reminder.

We are capable of rebirth. We are capable of being the most radiant bloom covered in scars, buried beneath layers of living. We are at the core…

Every shade of gray.

Katerina

Autumn leaves. The smell of pumpkin pie. The swirling of powdered sugar and cinnamon on the breeze. Words I am reading to you as you rest. Your breathing shallow and strained. But it comes. Inhale and exhale. Between each word I look to your chest to watch it rising and falling. Begging it to continue to do so. And then the knowledge of how much pain each breath brings. The strangeness that comes from wishing for one more breath and one last breath simultaneously.

I see you. Outside of your body. I see you there dancing. Your laugh bouncing off every heartbeat. I see your favorite pink dress. The way you twirled until the dizziness took hold. I feel your hand in mine as we fell to the earth together. Mesmerized by the sky, the wind, the stars, the moon.

I see your eyes and the way they always knew. Conversations start to play in my head on repeat.

You are illuminating light.

You are the endless love in every heart.

You are both the calm and the storm.

You are the butterfly and the flower.

The moon and the sun.

My Katerina you are eternal. You have become all of the fantastical characters we swooned over. You are immortal in your beauty. You are free.

By Night

The arch of her foot and the curves and edges of her waist.

The mahogany scar on her shoulder met by the steady gaze of ocean eyes that tell a story with every piece of light that radiated off them.

By night one discovers the details of human flesh illuminated by the beaming reflection of a midnight sky on a raging sea.

Details that get lost in the stark light of day.

The kiss on the side of her mouth when she smiles. The freckle on the tip of her nose.

I remember from touch more than sight. By the sound of her voice more than the movement of her lips. The aroma of rosemary from her hair…lingering still.

How well we loved…myself and I in the shrouded cover of nightfall.

Hands

Your skin was a lullaby. So different from my own. Soft and tender with rough edges that captivated.

You tasted like moonlight. Drippings of honey onto my lips.

Your hands made me forget the crescendo of pain throughout my body.

Each touch leading to another and with it a healing wherever your hands landed.

The needles that have been in my arms, the hands of doctors, the smell of hospitals fade.

All that is left is the sweet aroma of your skin. White sage in the rain. The beams of light hitting your hands as I run my fingers across every line and curve. Taking in every beauty mark.

Discovering all of your pieces and within them parts of my own that have been buried for too long.

You lit up the sea within me and held my hand as we danced along the star lit shore.

The Gift of Age

Lemon myrtle whispers on dew kissed skin. The heaviness of the sun ripened mango resting on the still air. As time moves fluidly, an ever flowing river, the flesh shifts, wilts and breathes new life.

Paint strokes around the eyes. Touches of silver in auburn hair. Disjointed pieces of a broken heart finding peace within an aging body.

Only when this temporary vessel starts to languish do we begin to understand the enduring nature of the soul. How the child like wonder can be found buried behind glittering eyes.

How flesh and bone are merely an illusion that our true self is borrowing, playing, experiencing.

When we look into faces we should see beating hearts and smiles that light a room with their grace. When we see laugh lines and hands hardened from labor and lives many burdens we should see stories, possibilities and the extraordinary beauty that exists in every imperfection.

Not all of us get to see our first silver locks. Too many come into this world flickering and they burn out before they even experience their first words. Not knowing the feeling of a lovers touch or what sheer heartbreaking awe you are left in when you love a child.

Too many will never see tomorrow and so we find gratitude in our own mortality. Find solace in the lack of knowing when we will leave this place. Find hope in the rhythm of the present. The gift of age may be the most incredible honor bestowed on anyone. Youth is divine but age means you have been granted the chance of life.

Live it dear one.

Connect

Tracing the curves of your skin is a habit I could never break.

My fingertips, tender on your lips knowing the smile they will provoke. Dimples on the right hand side as your mouth curls upwards.

Every scar from your childhood has become my own. The colors seeping from your eyes a mirror for every dream I have ever had.

This craving for human touch. Rooted deep within this ever transforming soul.

I want your bruises.

I want your beauty marks.

I want to feel your chest rising and falling beneath my hands.

I want it all.

These memories of flesh. These fleeting moments in a temporary body.

What is the point of being human?

To feel.

To feel every single thing this flicker of a life has to offer. To be mad with emotions. To linger on the sweetness of a kiss. To be transfixed by another souls journey. To recognize another being

With

One

Singular touch.

Why

Tell me why everything must die.

Each blossom only here for a flicker of time.

Every day of living bringing us closer to an end. Or is it a new beginning? The greatest adventure we have yet to know?

Why does music seep into our souls... the melodies so familiar? A million questions with no real answers. Perceptions. Ideas. Religions. Science. A flower to one is a weed to another.

Isn't there peace in that very knowledge?

That our heartbeats can align but our minds never will.

That the world will always be filled with an endless amount of questions and an even more endless amount of answers?

I don't believe we should ever stop asking why or searching for purpose in this existence... but we should take a moment and smile.

We will never know or see every answer. Just maybe we will become the answer. Some day in some place on some star. We will become.

Brotherhood

Two men looked on across the waterfalls of the unknown.

Rippling sunlight caught their steady gaze and engulfed them in a single moment of rapture within their reality of complete chaos.

Succumbing to the everyday sight, falling into the depths of their forgotten childhood imaginations.

Through crystallized eyes their hope was on an elusive high, as the brisk sense of luminescent euphoria embraced them at a least expecting time.

Machetes lie in scarlet pleasure and shine with a savage brilliance beneath the rising sun.

Names echo through the hills, names soon to be lost yet never forgotten.

The man made of coal stands gazing at the man made of clay and reaches his exhausted murderous hand, out across the barren lands feeling the souls of all who perished, within the one man who refused to die in the hands of his brother.

Papier-Mâché

Paper Faces painted with silken facades.
Pain a mere essence in the swift winds that are never seen nor
forgotten. Shades of a subtle grey outline the sky across the
motionless horizon of reality. Eyes scorn these pictures of
perfection, seeing nothing of love or loss, bearing in mind only a
fantasy of their own creation.

A girl made of porcelain stands alone drenched in the aura of
scarlet pleasure, betrayed and battered but a smile breaks her
tulip lips. She hums her life in simplistic descants of deceitful
desire. Lights descend upon the unwanted child; her eyes shine
through in a moment of truth to escape the bitter darkness of a
life based on a comely lie.

Ignorance weaved in with bliss, enraptured in the unconceivable
thought of imagining the impossible. Trapped inside this never
ending play, filled with thespians lashing out in the utmost
despair, begging to be saved from the torrid regret of a life with
no meaning.

The girl made of ceramic precision does not move from her bleeding place in the lie of life; she yearns to be felt, to experience something implausibly real…yet she dares not move. She can only witness the dulcet rhapsody of sinful covet, and can only watch as the people who are called criminals to God exhale pleasure in the utmost delight.

The light dims to a comfortable state, silence lurks behind the veneer of intelligent conversation leading nowhere. Condemned to bathe in euphoria of a believable flawlessness, forbidden to feel the ecstasy of veracity, she stands ever so still losing all plausible feeling, succumbing to the numbness she is bounded by. Her flowered mouth defeated by a pasted smile, turns into a reality as she flows with the motion of what has always been expected. For there is no escape for one who has never believed in anything except the mere essence of today.

The Soul of Sound

A pandemonium of music fills a small room full of lugubrious beings begging to never be seen.

Through all these woeful hearts, harmonious sounds trap condemned souls in a comely rapture of freedom.

Enraptured in complete rhapsody a young girl stands up, bloodshot night sky eyes holding a new found luminescent glory.

In fluid slow movements she relaxes her inhibited body, letting go of all she ever knew, flowing with the steady beats that repeated smoothly within her mind.

A boy sitting down in the darkness gapes at her with intoxicating desire. His eyes steadily fixed on her bodies graceful yet passionate motion, yearning to touch her flawless skin.

Never glancing once mesmerized in her own desires she kept on dancing, breathing fast transparent crystal air, escaping every possible affliction, losing herself in a phantasm of her own creation.

A fiery lust filled the room, any dismay that once took these people hostage had been swept away and replaced by torrid covet. The enduring beat played on moving souls to their own place in the music.

Free from tribulation, obscurity vanishing into oblivion locked in the lucid waves of mystic exhilarative sensation. Minds overtaken by rhythm, souls in a trance of enchantment, all caused by the music makers of the world.

Dynamite

Electricity.

Your touch awakening primal desires.

Achingly different from the safety of the mountains I have lived within.

You are the wildfire. The thunderstorm. The locrian mode in the midst of a composition.

One look.

Is all it took

For me to lose myself.

And to discover I had been sleeping all along.

And then with one gaze

Awakened with dynamite.

Wild Love

The most extraordinary moments of my life have happened
under darkness.

Bright light reminds me of hospitals.

Doctors.

Unanswered questions.

Flaring symptoms.

Burning skin.

But when the lights burn low. When the skies turn periwinkle
and the stars begin to peek out.

That is when wild love is born.

Where everything else is left in the light.

Sweet laughter.

Soft skin.

Sparkling eyes.

Reckless, unaffected, broken love.

Meet me at midnight.

Wild love.

Missing

Forever I felt a piece of my soul missing from me.

A quietness, a refuge, a calm inner knowing.

An acceptance of our mortality.

A breath deep, deeper than any of my short shallow cycles.

The moment I saw your eyes

Something was birthed within me.

Everything was ok. Everything was as it should be.

For the first time in my entire existence I took a breath in that I felt at the bottom of my chest.

A breath that awoke a wandering spirit, a quenching exhale of my endless fears.

So quickly you became part of my very being.

Then so slowly our love has burned, gently but powerfully like an eternal ember.

Sea, land and others attempted to severe the connection.

But every moment you were missing from me only pushed us against the current with more force.

You set my spirit free. You reminded me of my own wings.

You will forever be missing from me and I will hold my breath until I feel you presence once more.

Forever may our souls wander, intertwined in the stars.

Shallow

Tingling fingers and toes.

A heartbeat that doesn't know how to slow.

Eyes that are stunned. Lost. Overrun by fear.

Tight chest. Small, shallow breaths.

Not enough oxygen is making it around this broken body.

Panic.

Everyday a trigger. Everyday something new.

Illness makes these attacks come one after another.

Colliding. Magnifying. Escalating.

When the breathing mellows.

When the mind begins to level.

Exhaustion.

So deep, you curl into yourself.

Your eyes heavy. Too tired for tears.

Even rest can be painful.

When your days are spent navigating

A disquieted mind alongside an ailing body.

Shallow breathing.

Is how you're alive.

Let them come.

Curious and Curiouser

Days spent gazing out a closed window.

Longing to feel the warmth of the summer sun on bare skin.

Tasting the saltiness of the sea.

Needing to feel the raw earth beneath the arch of my feet.

A body that refuses to work is still a body.

Despite the limitations my mind is free.

There is a treasure in this knowledge.

A gift in a mind that is beaming with curiosity.

A mind that allows me to discover magnificence in every page.

That toils and researches for tomorrow.

Is able to find comedy in a painful reality.

There are parts of this splintered being that are worth it all.

Parts that keep me wanting…

For so much more.

The Space Between

There are times when I forget what it's like to be held by you.

Certain details are etched into the very core of my soul.

The shimmering green haze of your eyes in the sunlight.

The curve of your smile as I follow it time and time again

With my fingertips.

The sweet divots in your cheeks.

The smell of your skin that after times passage is synonymous
with the smell of home.

But other details are harder.

I know the feeling of your arms around my waist but then after
weeks pass, I can no longer feel them there.

The melancholy look as you read begins to fade.

And I sit, write and remember.

The pain of distance is overshadowed by the extraordinary beauty of seeing you after weeks, months even years apart.

A radiating joy that is akin to taking our very first breath.

A wailing scream that transforms into cries of release.

Our bodies always remember.

The mind needing time to pass before recollecting.

We continue.

Walking through love that is steeped in pain.

Our hearts fractured allowing exquisite grief to shine through.

The space between us can often feel insurmountable…

Then one touch…

One laugh…

One look…

One shared memory…

Love knows no distance. No boundaries. We dance between here and there. Making our way back to one another time and time again.

A Winter's Tale

Autumn leaves still falling.

Winter is beginning her journey.

The air is bitterly chilled, the smell of rain lingers in the early mornings.

The garden has come alive with passionfruit, guavas, butternut squash, thyme and rosemary.

Winter thyme making hearts skip beats.

The way it creeps through every crevice, growing large and strong.

The aroma dancing on the frosty wind.

Winter is a time to be born again.

It is a time for comfort.

Nourishment.

A woolen coat of warmth.

A gentle touch that reminds your soul you are not alone.

It is a time for returning home.

Dawn Meets Dusk

If you have been reading closely you will have noticed that a season happens to be missing from Dawn + Dusk.

Summer, Autumn and Winter are all accounted for but the bloom of Spring is strangely not present.

This is of course with the greatest intention. A meaning that will bind this book together.

The thread that you all know connects us to one another.

There was the dawn of my emotions and then at dusk, I found myself. I came together. I realized the beauty of our collective scars. The pain that touches so many of us.

As with all things there must be a meeting. No two people, places, experiences can go forever without at some point intersecting.

Welcome my dear ones to pages that explore the open parts of us…together. Words inspired by so many of you. Words from two sides of me becoming one. Words of recognition to all that have inspired me along the way.

This book is yours. These pages written for you.

You are part of my soul.

I love you.

The Grieving Heart

I am grieving.

A garden in need of tending.

Soil without nourishment.

Dry. Cold. Numb.

Earth unsuitable for growing.

I am grieving.

Yet at the same time I am growing life within me.

This paradox. This unrelenting pain.

My tears turn to wails. Screams of agony.

My understanding of the transition from life to death, birth to life. It does nothing to simmer the fragments of my heart.

No words could ever be enough. How do you tell a person all that they were to you on their deathbed?

How can you possibly communicate the essence of them that runs through your veins?

That occupies every fissure of your very being.

How can you say goodbye when you feel as though you just said hello?

I am grieving.

Differently every day. Acceptance followed by waves of begging the universe to give her back.

One more hug. One more look into her eyes. One more conversation.

Please, please let me just hear her voice.

She is the melody that gives me goosebumps.

The glimmering light that dances upon every surface right before the sun sets below the mountains.

She is my mother. My friend. She is your sister. Your lover. She is all of those we have lost and hold dear to us.

We are all grieving. We all will grieve.

This is the cycle of life.

The cycle of us.

Spring

She speaks in flowers.

I remember flowing cotton fabric, the smell of cilantro, doe brown eyes that always met mine with love.

The smell of eucalyptus on his skin. Lips that I had felt like I had known before, in another time, another life.

I remember the soft flesh of avocado speckled with pink salt crystals.

The way the sun lured out the green in his eyes, the sweet sound of wind through tall trees.

Hands tracing the edges of my face, memorizing the stars in my soul.

Defeated. Rejected. Scared. Alone.

Silence and his arms around my waist pulling me close and his voice saying... stay here with me.

I remember bits and pieces, fragments of whole photographs.

The painful moments blend gently like watercolor into the beautiful moments.

At times they all come flooding through my being and it is almost if I am made entirely of memories.

Bittersweet thoughts.

We will one day be nothing but a memory.

Our flesh, our breath will no longer be of this world.

One day our smell, our hair, the vibrancy of our eyes will only be engrained in the minds of those who experienced our living being.

In the same breadth, a privilege to be remembered.

And just as flowers bloom, we bloom and just as they wither, we wither.

Just as there is astounding beauty in blooming, there too exists extraordinary, breathtaking beauty in fading, in leaving this world just as we came into it.

Pandemonium

I ran to the waves just to feel the night in my hair.

The bitterly cold water rushing up my legs reminding me of the crimson blood coursing through my veins.

I chased the sliver of a moon through the trees, smelling the richness of pepper heavy on the air.

Freedom. The heaviness of pain, hurt, sorrow drifts away on the steady salt water…

And for a moment the suffocating chaos dissipates into a pandemonium of extraordinary beauty.

For a moment there is stillness and all I see is you shining in the light.

It is all I could ever need.

Skin

In the flash of the light leaving the horizon

Your skin became the only poetry

I never knew I needed.

Awake

Awakened.

The light seeped through the windows like golden honey.

Dripping slowly, sweetly onto porcelain flesh.

The light found the scars, it illuminated them from the shadows.

The desire to run back into the darkness ceased and my body
collapsed

Bathing in the warmth I had hidden from for my whole
existence.

Wait

I waited for my soul today.

I found pieces that had been missing along the way.

In the pulsating life of nature

I began to find myself.

Contradiction

And if I could describe exactly what my soul feels like it would
be

The ocean and the forest colliding.

A contradiction.

A meeting of two not like the other.

Chaos

Fury

Black holes

Of depth that have yet to be understood.

Calm

A place of pulsating life.

Sturdy.

Enduring.

Movement and stillness all in one breadth.

La Luna

You know when the moon is at her fullest and her light streams down on the ocean like one million stars cascading from the night sky?

A thousand kisses to calm the chaotic beauty of the sea.

She is the very chaos.

The passion, the love and the tenderness.

If you look close enough you will see her smile

Striking and endearing

Shining back at you.

Amani

She was a woman that could not be held down, could not be captured.

Rather she was a woman that had to be loved like the seasons, never still always moving.

Her favorite fruit was pineapple.

Her favorite color purple.

He knew everything about her before he even knew her name.

Dear Life

The soul dances on the stars and wonders.

A whispy cloud floating on a light blue sky with beams of light breaking through.

An ethereal beauty with raven hair and eagle eyes, an evergreen rooted deeply in rich earth.

What life will I join with? What journey will I embark on?

Will I know the feeling of a heart beating inside?

Or will I feel the wind and smell the soil of many different lands?

Will I still be enamored by the color pink?

Will I be made of lightness and darkness, sunshine and storms?

Or will my very essence alter and change, forever in a cyclical transformation?

Will I know what it feels like to beat my wings against the breeze?

Or will I be strong, steady and become polished from the roaring gentle strength of water?

To live is to die. To die is to live.

In the Orchard

The Apple Orchard was cloaked in an ethereal mist. The kind that wraps around your body leaving the smallest dew drops on your arms.

An intoxicating aroma of sweetness lingering on every inhale. The sun was still in hibernation, the sky speckled with purple and blue. The quiet broken by the sound of creatures coming alive and slowly stretching their sleeping bones.

Walking through these lines of trees will forever bring me back to the ephemeral moments of childhood wonder.

Times before my body knew what illness was.

Times before anxiety became a loyal companion.

Times before I had any concept of the fragility of life.

A time when time itself had no bearing on my life.

When the smallest trinket was the greatest pleasure.

When I measured my days by the amount of laughter, the pinecones and berries in my basket, the sticky sweetness of apples on my lips.

In the midst of the chaos and enduring hardships of adulthood, a body that ails, forever goodbyes and the grief that accompanies them... I go back to the orchard.

Sometimes I lie on the cold, wet Earth. I stare upward to the dark clouds and twinkling stars then watch them fade into the orange blossom of sunset.

I tell myself that in this singular moment all is well.

All will be as it should.

Closing my eyes and breathing in the fruits of life.

Bruised Fruit

Bruised fruit. At markets it's often disposed of or sold for a fraction of the price.

People pick an apple, a lemon, a peach if it has marks or scars they have a tendency to instantly put it back down.

Searching with precision for perfection.

Have you ever tried a peach, bruised and battered fresh off the tree?

Warm from the sunshine beating down, the sweetness is a memory that withstands the cruelty of time.

When I see injured fruit I see immortal beauty.

No different than when I see battered souls.

Their spirts even when hidden down in the caverns of survival, they peek through.

There is an unrelenting comeliness in those that endure.

A grace. A smile that stops you in your tracks.

To smile when nothing is ok…the power that lingers in that.

I am a deeply flawed and broken individual.

I have bruises, scars, marks and wounds from the illness I carry and from the life I have lived.

I can tell you one of the foremost magnificent moments of my life…

My love wrapping me in his arms and kissing each one as if their very existence made him fall in love with me.

Our brokenness, our weakness, our downfalls…they make us perfect.

They are the remnants of a life lived and experienced.

Reminders of the times our bodies and hearts held on for dear life.

A sonnet that speaks of compassion, endurance, bravery and unfaltering courage.

Next time you are at the market, I urge you to pick the dimpled lemon, the bruised apple, the peach with brown spots…

I urge you to fall in love with imperfection.

To taste the sweetness of

Bruised Fruit.

An Ode to the Broken

A soul of a wanderer is in continuous desire for more. More love, more passion, more pain, more pleasure, more tears, more laughter, more moments of poignant beauty. Always needing something new, something extraordinary. These souls are magnificent and in turmoil all at once. When I was younger I yearned for everything. I was sick with curiosity, driven by a need to see every single thing the world had to offer.

As I grew and experienced the harder lessons like illness and loss I began to realize what a privilege my life of wandering had been.

It is imperative to wonder. It is essential to have imagination and drive to live your life as fully as possible.

But it is also a gift to know the preciousness of this exact moment, no matter how mundane. If your day is filled with blankets and dreams of a better tomorrow. That's ok. If you are fighting with your beloved, or feeling like goodbye is inevitable. Breathe in. Breathe out. Know that whatever is meant to be will be. Never turn yourself off to love because of fear.

I cannot stress enough. Travel, adventure, job opportunities... they come and they go.

People... people are fragile. You are on borrowed time loving them. Remember that. Pull them into you. Don't let go. If you want to run free, hold their hand and let them run with you. Each and every moment with the people you love is irreplaceable.

The moon is rising. Stars are out tonight. The ocean is gentle with a smoky horizon. My face is turning to ice from the almost winter wind. And in this quiet moment of everyday there is only gratitude in my heart. Somehow despite it all I'm still here.

If you are reading this. You are here too. And you are enough. As you are. Discover the world, meet people, fall in love... but also know that without all of it... you are still enough. One bite of bliss is more than most get in a whole lifetime.

Savor it my dear hearts. Savor it all.

Love you to the moon and stars,

Michelle

Michelle Gerrard-Marriott lives in Ojai, California. She is enchanted by the midnight sky. She wakes with dusk and rests with the sunrise. The water is another home. Horses some of her closest friends. She left pieces of her soul in Kenya, Australia and England. She yearns to feel all forms of love and to give love at every possible turn.

www.ingramcontent.com/pod-product-compliance
Lightning Source LLC
Chambersburg PA
CBHW021911040426
42447CB00007B/809